Zoey
the
Christmas Kitty

Dawn Smith Jordan
Illustrated by Rebecca Parfitt

XULON PRESS

Xulon Press
2301 Lucien Way #415
Maitland, FL 32751
407.339.4217
www.xulonpress.com

Illustrator: Rebecca Parfitt
Editor: Sue McLeese
Co-editor: Allison Hodge

Paperback ISBN-13: 978-1-66285-913-7

DEDICATION

This book is dedicated to anyone who has loved and lost their faithful companion, with the promise there is another waiting just for you.

ANIMAL SHELTER

This is the story of Zoey the Christmas Kitty.

Mommy's favorite time of year, Christmas, was just around the corner. Mommy loved everything about Christmas. She loved baking, decorating, caroling, shopping for gifts, wrapping presents and visiting family. But this Christmas would be different, because her beloved kitty, Skunky, had recently gone to kitty heaven. Both Mommy and her dog, Cookie, missed him very much. Skunky had always loved the Christmas treats Mommy made especially for him, but now there was no need for Mommy to make them. After a few weeks, she decided it was time to go to the animal shelter and find a new kitty to adopt. Mommy walked around, looking at all the adorable kittens up for adoption. As she peered into a cage in the last row, a little, yellow striped paw reached out to touch her face. It was love at first sight. Mommy felt sure this was the kitten for her. She told the lady at the shelter she had to go out of town for the weekend, but would be back first thing Monday morning to bring him home. She gave the yellow striped kitten a final hug and left.

On Monday morning, Mommy called the lady at the shelter to tell her she was on the way to adopt her new kitty. However, the lady told her that over the weekend a little girl and her parents had come to the shelter. Just like Mommy, the little girl had fallen in love with the yellow striped kitty. And just like Mommy's, this little girl's kitty had also gone to kitty heaven. Her parents explained the little girl was sick and couldn't go to school. She was homeschooled, and the kitty had been her best friend, her special playmate and her secret sharer. Without her friend, the little girl was lonely. The lady at the shelter said she knew Mommy would understand, and she let the family take the kitten home.

ANIMAL SHELTER

While Mommy understood and was glad the kitten and the girl had found each other, she was still very sad. She, too, had loved that yellow kitten. But the lady at the shelter said she had another kitten she wanted Mommy to see, one that very badly needed someone to love her. When Mommy walked into the shelter, the lady lifted a tiny, six-weeks-old black and white kitten from the back of a cage. She was not beautiful like the yellow striped kitten. She was terribly skinny, and her eyes were matted and closed. But, as Mommy listened to the story of the black and white kitten, her heart began to soften.

The tiny black and white kitten had been part of a litter of feral, meaning wild, kittens born under a lady's house, with the mother cat nowhere to be found. The lady called the animal shelter to come rescue the litter, which they promptly did, catching all the kittens except the black and white one. Running around in circles, she couldn't seem to find her way out from beneath the house. When she finally stumbled out, they realized at once she was blind. All the kittens were taken back to the animal shelter where, one by one, her brothers and sisters were adopted. No one wanted the blind kitten. She was so tiny, her eyes were closed and matted with infection and she lay very still. But the director of the shelter would not give up on her. She named her Hope, and every morning when she arrived at the shelter, she would call for Hope. But Hope did not look in her direction, remaining sad and uninterested. Still, the lady at the shelter was persistent, believing there was still hope for her. She prayed every day that God would heal her eyes and help her to see. She put drops of medicine in her eyes every day, always praying as she did.

One morning, when she came in for work, like every other morning she called for Hope. And on this day, the little black and white kitten looked right at her. The lady excitedly asked, "Hope, can you see me?" And as she stepped first left and then right, the kitten's eyes followed her. With tears in her eyes, the lady called Mommy. It was a miracle. She could see! God had answered her prayer. How happy and thankful both Mommy and the lady were.

When Mommy saw the skinny, cloudy-eyed kitten, she gently picked her up, still unsure if this sickly kitten was the one for her. Immediately, the little black and white kitten snuggled under her chin, began to loudly purr and, with a sigh, rested her head against Mommy's shoulder. She licked Mommy's chin and nose, and Mommy knew in that instant that this was the kitten God meant for her. So, she took her home.

Mommy continued to put the drops of medicine in her eyes until the day came when Hope no longer needed them. Her eyes were clear, and she could see. She was a happy, healthy, playful little girl, and Mommy's family was once again complete. She had settled into her "fur-ever" home with Mommy and Cookie. Mommy decided Hope needed a new name. One day, Mommy's grown daughter came to visit. Upon hearing the story of the black and white kitten, she exclaimed, "Her name should be Zoey! It means life." And so it was settled. Zoey's name suited her well, as she was very lively, getting into everything! And this is how the adventures of Zoey the Christmas kitty began!

As Christmas grew even nearer, Mommy brought out the Christmas tree. Watching closely, Zoey's eyes grew very big. She was fascinated with this giant new toy, full of bright colored lights and shiny ornaments. At first, she stayed under the Christmas tree, looking up into it, completely still. And then, to Mommy's surprise, Zoey climbed up on the bottom branch, then the next one, and the next, and before Mommy knew it, she had climbed all the way to the top of the Christmas tree! Staring down proudly from the top, it was as if Zoey were laying claim to the new fun toy and announcing, "This tree is mine!"

No matter how many times Mommy said, "No, Zoey!" and took her down, Zoey would climb right back up the branches again and again and again. She loved the Christmas tree, always wanting to be in the very top of it! That first night, Mommy went to bed, but Zoey did not follow her as she usually did. The next morning, when Mommy walked into the living room, every single red ball and all the ornaments she had so carefully hung on the Christmas tree were now scattered all over the floor. Zoey had knocked them all off! Mommy laughed at her mischievous little girl and put all the ornaments back on the tree. The next morning, it was the same thing. The ornaments were scattered all over the floor, while Miss Zoey stared down from the top branch. Mommy laughed again. She had a very busy little girl. After many nights of the same thing, Mommy decided she would just leave the decorations off the Christmas tree this year, and Zoey happily spent the holidays perched from her favorite place on the branches, looking down on Mommy and Cookie.

When Mommy's son and daughter came home for Christmas, they asked why all the beautiful ornaments were not on the Christmas tree? Mommy explained how Zoey would knock them all off each night, and they all laughed. As they opened gifts together on Christmas Eve and morning, Zoey watched from high up in the tree as if to say, "I am the star on top of this tree!" She was most certainly even more adorable than the elegant angel that traditionally sat on the top branch.

When Christmas was over, Zoey could not understand why Mommy was taking down her favorite toy. She would not let Mommy put the final branches into the big red storage container, hanging onto them with her tiny paws. So, Mommy decided to leave the Christmas tree up, just for Zoey, by moving it to the basement so she could happily sit in her favorite place!

While Mommy's Christmas tree was not as beautiful as it had always been every Christmas before Zoey came, it held a different beauty. It was the miracle of Christmas love that transformed an unwanted little kitten into a beautiful, happy-go-lucky kitty, who perfectly completed Mommy's family. Instead of being decorated with shiny red and gold balls and brightly colored keepsake ornaments, it held something more treasured. Mommy realized the best Christmas gift of all was the sweet little kitty perched happily in the branches of her tree. Mommy had learned an important lesson. Sometimes the gifts we hope for don't come in the packages we thought they would. While Mommy had thought the little yellow striped kitten was the perfect one for her, she had come to realize the little black and white kitty whom nobody else wanted had been saved just for her. Even when we are sure we know just what we want or need, our Heavenly Father knows us better than we know ourselves. His gifts are always perfect. And do you know what happened? Zoey, the Christmas kitty, loved Christmas just as much as Mommy did! God knew all along that this was the very kitty Mommy needed, just as much as the little black and white kitty needed Mommy. *And so, the adventures of Zoey the Christmas kitty had only just begun. . .*

"Every good and perfect gift is from above, coming down from the Father." James 1:7

Rebecca Parfitt, Illustrator
Sue McLeese, Editor
Allison Hodge, Co-editor

CPSIA information can be obtained
at www.ICGtesting.com
Printed in the USA
JSHW032103221022
31885JS00003B/4